JOSEPH HAYDN

GW00734017

PASSION
The Seven Words of our Saviour on the Cross

Vocal Score

Novello

PREFACE.

ABOUT fifteen years ago I was applied to by a Clergyman at Cadiz, and requested to write instrumental music to the Seven Words of JESUS on the Cross.

It was then customary every year, during Lent, to perform an Oratorio in the Cathedral at Cadiz, the effect of which the following arrangements contributed to heighten. The walls, windows, and columns of the Church were hung with black cloth, and only one large lamp, hanging in the centre, lighted the solemn and religious gloom. At noon all the doors were closed, and the music began. After a prelude, suited to the occasion, the Bishop ascended the Pulpit, and pronounced one of the Seven Words, which was succeeded by reflections upon it. As soon as these were ended, he descended from the Pulpit and knelt before the Altar. The pause was filled by music. The Bishop ascended and descended again a second, a third time, and so on; and each time the Orchestra filled up the intervals in the discourse.

My Composition must be judged on a consideration of these circumstances. The task of writing seven *Adagios*, each of which was to last about ten minutes, to preserve a connection between them without wearying the hearers, was none of the lightest; and I soon found that I could not confine myself within the limits of the time prescribed.

The music was originally without text, and was printed in that form. It was only at a later period that I was induced to add the text.

The Oratorio entitled " The Seven Words of Our Redeemer on the Cross," as a complete and, as regards the vocal parts, an entirely new work, was first published by Messrs. BREITKOPF & HÄRTEL, of Leipsic.

The partiality with which this work has been received by scientific Musicians leads me to hope that it will not be without effect on the public at large.

JOSEPH HAYDN.

Vienna, March, 1801.

Stand when conductor & soloists enter
Sit when soloists exit

INTRODUCTION.

2

No. 1.

CHORAL.—"FATHER, FORGIVE THEM."

Luke xxiii. 34.

CHORUS.—"LAMB OF GOD."

6

- flic - ted, O Lamb . . . of God.

- flic - ted, O Lamb . . . of God.

- flic - ted, O Lamb . . . of God.

- flic - ted, O Lamb . . . of God.

But Thou didst no vi - o - lence, nor was de -

But Thou didst no vi - o - lence, nor was de -

Thou didst no vi - o - lence, nor was de -

Thou didst no vi - o - lence, nor was de -

- ceit in Thy mouth.

- ceit in Thy mouth.

- ceit in Thy mouth.

- ceit in Thy mouth.

21

NOV070163

No. 3.   CHORAL.—" WOMAN, BEHOLD."   John xix. 26, 27.

CHORUS.—" DAUGHTERS, WEEP NOT."

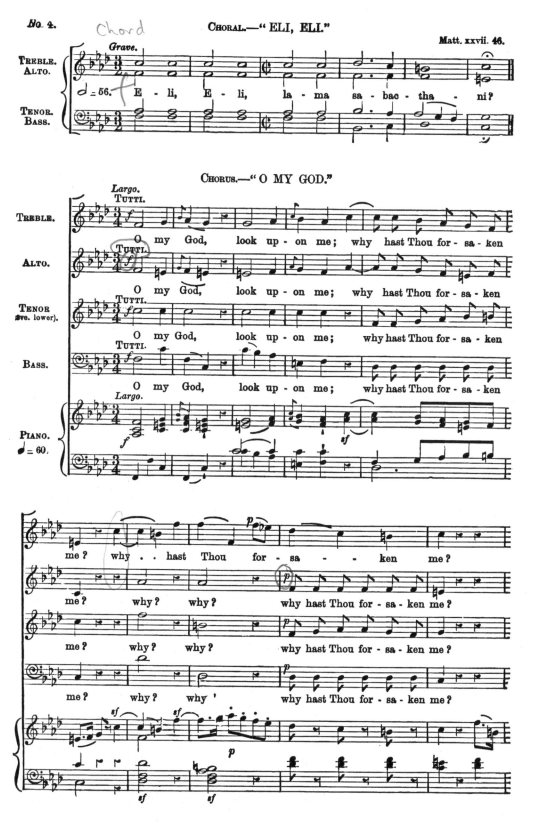

S1 Tonsignal

stand on signal

No. 5.

"I THIRST."

John xix. 28

60

NOV070163

No. 7. Chord Choral.—" **FATHER, INTO THY HANDS.**"

Luke xxiii. 46.

Chorus.—" **INTO THY HANDS, O LORD.**"

THE EARTHQUAKE.

slept a - rose, a - rose. . . . .

slept a - rose, a - rose. . . .

slept a - rose, a - rose. . .

slept a - rose, a - rose.

The earth did quake, the rocks were rent;

The earth did quake, the rocks were rent;

The earth did quake, the rocks were rent;

The earth did quake, the rocks were rent;

for tru - ly this was the Son of God, . . . whose

for tru - ly this was the Son of God, . . . whose

for tru - ly this was the Son of God, . . . whose

for tru - ly this was the Son of God, . . . whose

Printed in Great Britain 7/06(59187).

INDEX.

No.				PAGE
	INTRODUCTION			1
1.	CHORAL	Father, forgive them		4
	CHORUS WITH SOLI ...	Lamb of God		4
2.	CHORAL	Verily, I say unto Thee		13
	CHORUS WITH SOLI ...	Lord, have mercy		13
3.	CHORAL	Woman, behold thy son		23
	CHORUS WITH SOLI ...	Daughters, weep not		23
4.	CHORAL	Eli, Eli, lama sabachthani ?		34
	CHORUS WITH SOLI ...	O my God, look upon me		34
	INTERMEZZO			44
5.	CHORUS WITH SOLI ...	I thirst		46
6.	CHORAL	It is finished		56
	CHORUS WITH SOLI ...	It is finished		56
7.	CHORAL	Father, into Thy hands		65
	CHORUS WITH SOLI ...	Into Thy hands, O Lord		65
	CHORUS	The Earthquake...		74